THE OFFICIAL SCOTLAND FOOTBALL ANNUAL 2009

Written by Roddy Mackenzie

Contributors: Graeme Booth, Michael Mackenzie, Al Watt

A Grange Publication

© 2008. Published by Grange Communications Ltd., Edinburgh, under licence from The Scottish Football Association. Printed in the EU.

Photographs by © SNSPix, The Scottish FA, The Scottish Football Museum

ISBN 978-1-906211-58-5

£6.99

CONTENTS

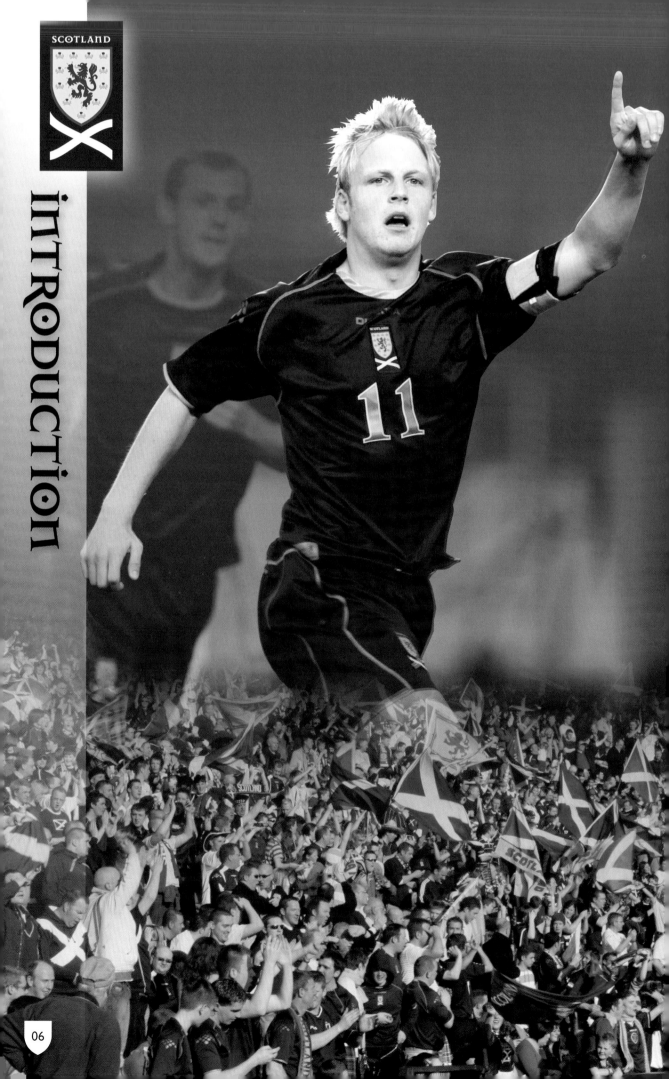

SCOTLAND

introduction

What was Scotland's greatest game? It is a debate that will both divide and unite the Tartan Army with the merits of this match or that match. Scotland have, after all, beaten England 5-1 at Wembley, and World Cup finalists France home and away. They even managed to win against Germany away from home, and against Argentina at Hampden, albeit in friendly matches.

Our Top Five is sure to spark the debate as fans argue over what they see as glaring omissions or certain games they believe are unworthy of making the final count.

But it is this sort of debate that has fuelled the Tartan Army down through the years and made them one of the most passionate supports to follow any nation. Wherever a Scotland team plays (and even sometimes when they don't!), there will be a saltire or a lion rampant dancing in the crowd.

As Scotland embarks on a new era under George Burley and seeks to make it to the 2010 World Cup finals in South Africa, it is a time to acknowledge our rich heritage but also to look to the future.

One thing's for sure – it will never be dull!

GEORGE BURLEY A-Z

Scotland manager George Burley is relishing the opportunity to guide the national side and the different challenges it offers after managing at club level. Here we look back at a few significant landmarks in his career.

A is for Ayr United - George had his first break in coaching when he spent three years in charge at Somerset Park.

B is for Best – George was in direct opposition to George Best when he made his Ipswich Town debut against Manchester United.

C is for Cumnock – the town where George was born on June 3, 1956.

D is for Derby – George took over the reins at Derby County in 2003, initially on a short-term contract but was then given a two-year deal.

E is for Europe – George helped Ipswich Town win the UEFA Cup in 1981 but unfortunately missed the two-leg final against AZ Alkmaar due to injury.

F is for Fir Park – George signed for Motherwell in 1985 after returning north of the border and had two spells with the Fir Park club.

G is for Gillingham – George's last port of call as a player in England before returning north.

H is for Hearts – George had a successful but brief management spell at Tynecastle as he guided the team to the top of the SPL.

I is for Ipswich Town – where George served with distinction both as a player and manager.

J is for Jankauskas – Edgaras Jankauskas was recruited by Burley when he was at Tynecastle and the Lithuanian striker was highly rated in Europe.

K is for Kilmarnock – George's first competitive match as Hearts' manager was a 4-2 win at Rugby Park which set the team on their unbeaten run.

L is for League Managers' Association – Named Manager of the Year in 2001 by the League Managers' Association after guiding Ipswich to fifth place in the Premiership and a UEFA Cup place.

M is for Maradona – George won his fourth cap as a teenage Maradona turned on the style at Hampden, scoring in a 3-1 friendly win for Argentina.

N is for Northern Ireland – George celebrated his first Scotland win as a late goal from Arthur Graham led to a 1-0 win over the Irish in a Home International match in May, 1979.

O is for Osborne – Roger Osborne scored the only goal of the 1978 FA Cup final as Ipswich beat Arsenal 1-0 and George celebrated at Wembley.

P is for Pressley – Steven Pressley formed a close bond with George at Hearts and was taken on as part of the Scotland coaching team.

Q is for Quest – George hopes to lead Scotland to a major finals for the first time in 12 years as the World Cup campaign gathers momentum.

R is for Robson – Sir Bobby Robson was a huge influence on George's career when he started out at Ipswich.

S is for Sunderland – George left Ipswich in 1985 and signed for Sunderland.

T is for Tony – Tony Mowbray was one of George's signings at Ipswich and he went on to become assistant manager of the club under him.

U is for Uncle – George's nephew Craig followed him into the Scotland team and played in the last World Cup finals that Scotland qualified for in 1998.

V is for Vladimir – Vladimir Romanov brought George back to Scottish football to manage Hearts but there was a parting of the ways a few months later.

W is for Wales – George made his international debut against Wales at Ninian Park in 1979 but John Toshack scored a hat-trick to give the home side a 3-0 win.

X is for X-rated – One of George's lowest points as a manager came when Ipswich lost 9-0 to Manchester United at Old Trafford in 1995 with Andy Cole scoring five.

Y is for Youth – George was a product of Ipswich's celebrated youth system as he joined the club straight from school.

Z is for Zero – The number of SPL matches George lost during his time as Hearts' manager.

SCOTLAND

Scotland have a long and tricky road to negotiate if they are to make it to the World Cup finals in South Africa in 2010. Here we take a look at the countries that stand in the way.

FYR Macedonia

Home stadium:
City Stadium, Skopje

FIFA ranking:
54

Head coach:
Srecko Katanec

Top club:
FK Rabotniki

Biggest win:
Liechtenstein 1 Macedonia 11 (9.11.1996)

Worst defeat:
Macedonia 0 Belgium 5 (7.6.1995)

Most capped player:
Goce Sedloski (84)

Star player:
Goran Pandev – 25-year-old Lazio striker

World Cup record:
never qualified

Fascinating fact:
Macedonian Pece Atanasovski won the top award at the World Bagpipe Festival in Sicily in 1968 beating 1800 bagpipers from around the world.

Norway

Home stadium:
Ullevaal Stadium, Oslo

FIFA ranking:
29

Head coach:
Åge Hareide

Top club:
SK Brann

Biggest win:
Norway 12 Finland 0 (28.6.1946)

Worst defeat:
Denmark 12 Norway 0 (7.10.1917)

Most capped player:
Thorbjørn Svenssen (104)

Star player:
Steffen Iverson – scored against Scotland in 2004 has over 70 caps

World Cup record:
qualified in 1938, 1994 and 1998 reaching the second round in '98

Fascinating fact:
The Norwegian national team is the only team that has played Brazil and never lost to them.

Iceland

Home stadium:
Laugardalsvollur, Reykjavik

FIFA ranking:
97

Head coach:
Ólafur Jóhannesson

Top club:
Valur

Biggest win:
Iceland 9 Faroe Islands 0 (10.6.1985)

Worst defeat:
Denmark 14 Iceland 2 (23.8.1967)

Most capped player:
Rúnar Kristinsson (104)

Star player:
Eidur Gudjohnsen – captain and leading scorer with over 20 goals for his country

World Cup record:
never qualified

Fascinating fact:
In a friendly match against Estonia in April 1997 Iceland became the first international team to have a father and son play in the same match as Eidur Gudjohnsen came on as substitute for his father Arnor.

Netherlands

Home stadium:
Amsterdam ArenA, De Kuip, Rotterdam Philips Stadion, Eindhoven

FIFA ranking:
4

Head coach:
Bert van Marwijk

Top club:
PSV Eindhoven

Biggest win:
Netherlands 9 - 0 Norway (1.11.1972)

Worst defeat:
England Amateur 12 - 2 Netherlands (21.12.1907)

Most capped player:
Edwin van der Sar (125)

Star player:
Arjen Robben – winger has won league titles with PSV, Chelsea and Real Madrid.

World Cup record:
Eight appearances. Beaten finalists in 1974 and 1978, finished fourth in 1998.

Fascinating fact:
Over the years the Dutch national team has been managed by 15 Englishmen. The first was Edgar Chadwick from 1908 to 1913. The last was George Hardwick in 1957.

SCOTLAND

Julie Fleeting MBE has achieved something her male counterparts are unlikely to equal – scoring 100 goals for her country. Since taking up the game at the age of nine, she has gone on to become a role-model for girls wanting to play the game in Scotland. Her career, which has seen her win over 100 caps for her country, has seen her play for Ayr United, Ross County, San Diego Spirit and Arsenal.

Julie Fleeting has come a long way since she first started playing football for Cunningham Boys' Club at the age of nine. The women's game in Scotland has grown up with her.

As a nine year-old, she could not find a girls' team to play for and had to play alongside boys for four years. Now, girls' teams are springing up all over the country in what is one of the biggest growth areas for the game.

To show how much progress the game has made since Fleeting started out, there are now 56 senior women's teams in the Scottish Leagues. The Women's A Squad, run by Sweden's Anna Signeul - who succeeded Vera Pauw from the Netherlands, currently has a FIFA World Ranking of 26 and this year the Scotland Under-19 girls' team reached the Finals of the UEFA European Women's U19 Championships in France, but lost their three matches (to Sweden 2-1, England 3-1 and Germany 7-0).

There is now an established Under-17 girls' squad and the recruiting process mirrors the selection process for boys' youth squads.

Fleeting is excited to see the way the game has developed but she knows there is still some way to go if Scotland is to be on a level playing field with countries such as Germany, America and Norway.

She acknowledges that, while the game is growing in Scotland as it becomes more professional, it is the work of volunteer coaches that has laid the foundations.

"When I started playing for Prestwick who then became Ayr United, we had players coming from all over the country – from Dundee, Motherwell, Coatbridge and Stirling – but we were fortunate to have girls who were really committed to playing," Fleeting recalls.

"We also had a great coach in Hugh Flynn. It's people like him that keep the game going in Scotland. If it hadn't been for his dedication and willingness to give up his spare time to coach players then I would never have had the opportunities that I had.

When you're older, you realise what people have given up to run teams and how much work they have put into the game."

Fleeting, a PE teacher at Auchenharvie Academy in Stevenston, Ayrshire, underlines that players need to work harder than ever before if they are to reach the top in the women's game and play for their country.

"There are so many more players now to choose from than when I first started playing for Scotland. There are now teams all over the country and the competition for places is a lot more intense than it was before," she outlines.

FLEETING
100

A FLEETING moment

"Players have to work that bit harder to earn an international cap, although I'm not saying it was easy when I first played as you had to give up a lot.

When I first started playing for Ayr United, it wasn't as if they were just around the corner. I had to travel half-an-hour to training and half-an-hour back and it also meant a commitment from my parents to take me there and bring me back.

At 14-15, it is an age where there are outside pressures on girls and there are difficult decisions to be taken.

I was fortunate at Ayr United in that we were all pretty dedicated and would socialise together and we all helped each other so that we weren't dragged in different directions.

We worked hard together and we knew that we had to make sacrifices on the social side if we wanted to continue to play at a high level.

It's different for female players. When boys start playing in the street, they dream of playing for one of the professional clubs.

I never thought of it that way as I never thought there would be a day when I would be paid for playing football.

I just enjoyed the game and played as much as I could and did not really think of where it would take me.

That's why playing in America was such a great opportunity. To live in San Diego and get paid for playing was just something I never expected.

It was a shame the league didn't last. It maybe grew

too fast when there weren't sufficient sponsors and players were maybe getting paid too much.

But I know there are plans to try and revive it and they will learn from any mistakes that were made the last time.

I don't see a professional league happening in Scotland during my playing time. Maybe there will be a semi-professional league but I think we're still some way away from having professional clubs.

Just now, there are a lot of sacrifices. Players are working all day but must then find the energy to go out and train five times a week, it's not easy.

You cannot have the same social side of your life that other people have and I've been fortunate that I'm from a football family and they understand the commitment.

There are times when I don't feel like training but my husband (goalkeeper Colin Stewart) will always encourage me to go out as he knows what I have to do."

Fleeting underlines that playing for Scotland brings with it a responsibility as you are setting an example for others to follow.

"I think any player that is in the national team is a role model for young players. You have to have the correct lifestyle and you don't want to throw the opportunity away," she stresses.

"There are no easy games now in international football. There are a lot of good countries now in Europe - Germany and Scandinavia have always been strong - but other countries are also improving fast.

In Norway, national team players are given around £2,000 a month so they can live like a professional and not have to work full-time.

In other countries, players have part-time jobs and train for the rest of the day and it would be great if Scotland could move more in that direction."

And, in conclusion, Fleeting's advice for any young player starting out who wants to go on and play for Scotland.

"You have to enjoy the game, first and foremost. You have to work really hard at your game in training and you have to listen to the coaches and have respect for them. They are giving up a lot of time and effort for you and that has to be respected, you have to give something back in return. There are a lot of young girls taking up the game now and, if they go along to a team and don't get a game right away, then they should keep working at it.

Football is all about chances and sometimes the best ones happen when you least expect them.

You have to have dedication to succeed but it's also about getting the balance right in your life.

If you just play football all the time, you can become bored with it after a year and end up giving up the game.

You have to make time for your friends and for the likes of going to the cinema and, above all, you must be happy."

SCOTLAND

POSITIONAL QUIZ

What is your strongest position? See how you measure up with our Scotland positional quiz.

Goalkeepers

1   Who is Scotland's most-capped goalkeeper?

2   Only two goalkeepers have won more than 50 caps for Scotland – who are they?

3   Who was Scotland's goalkeeper in the 1974 World Cup finals in Germany?

4   Which goalkeeper famously lost nine goals against England in a match at Wembley in 1961?

5   Who was the last goalkeeper to play for Scotland in a European Championships finals?

Defenders

6   Who is Scotland's most-capped defender?

7   Richard Gough won 61 caps for Scotland while he was playing for which three club sides?

8   Which defender had the misfortune to score an own goal against Brazil in the World Cup opener at France '98?

9   How many caps did Colin Hendry win for Scotland?

10   Which player scored Scotland's winner against France in the Euro 2008 qualifier at Hampden?

Midfield players

11   Who won more international caps for Scotland – Billy Bremner or Graeme Souness?

12   Who is Scotland's most-capped midfield player?

13   Who did Barry Ferguson make his international debut against?

14   Which midfield player scored twice in Scotland's 5-2 win over New Zealand in the 1982 World Cup finals?

15   Who scored Scotland's last goal at a World Cup finals?

Strikers

16   Which striker scored Scotland's only goal at Euro '96?

17   Who did Kenny Dalglish win his last international cap against?

18   How many World Cup finals tournaments did Denis Law play in?

19   Who did Joe Jordan make his international debut against?

20   How many goals did Colin Stein score against Cyprus in a World Cup qualifier at Hampden in 1969?

Answers on page 61

N	O	R	E	H	C	T	E	L	F	R
W	N	L	Y	H	A	R	T	L	E	Y
O	M	E	M	H	T	W	M	U	R	L
I	I	W	D	T	U	H	C	Y	G	L
M	L	D	N	D	F	T	F	E	U	E
F	L	B	O	D	A	G	T	L	S	W
T	E	O	D	N	B	F	T	O	O	D
Y	R	Y	R	G	W	N	C	H	N	L
R	O	C	O	N	N	O	R	M	D	A
A	J	F	G	U	S	H	R	H	U	C
H	Y	M	I	L	L	N	N	B	T	R

Find these current Scotland players in the word-search (names can go diagonal, vertical, horizontal or backwards)

1.	HUTTON	6.	OCONNOR
2.	GORDON	7.	MCFADDEN
3.	FERGUSON	8.	CALDWELL
4.	HARTLEY	9.	FLETCHER
5.	MILLER	10.	BROWN

Solution on Page 61

17

A look back to Scotland's bold bid to reach 2008 as the team – led by firstly Walter Smith and then Alex McLeish – shook World Champions Italy and runners-up France in a tale of the unexpected...

After the qualifying draw for the European Championships was made, few would have given Scotland a haggis's chance on Burns' Night of making the finals in Austria and Switzerland. Those of that view were ultimately proved correct; but only after a campaign which re-ignited the pride in the national team.

A Team Re-Born

It had been eight years since Scotland had reached a major finals when Walter Smith and his team set about the monumental task of qualification for Euro 2008. Before them lay the two sides that had contested the World Cup Final just a matter of months before, as well as quarter-finalists Ukraine. Of the 'lesser' teams in the group, both Lithuania and the Faroe Islands had taken points from Scotland in earlier campaigns and Georgia, managed by the experienced Klaus Toppmoller, could not be discounted.

Morale-boosting wins over the Faroe Islands and Lithuania in September 2006 got the Scots off to a perfect start. A month later and it was three wins out of three - victory over France at Hampden left the Tartan Army daring to dream. The fantastic rearguard display against the French gave Scotland one of the proudest moments in the nation's footballing history.

After surviving a first half of French domination, the spirit of the Scottish side seemed to take almost human form. There were 25 minutes to survive after Gary Caldwell had scored, but with a group playing as they did for each other, the outcome should not have been in doubt. When, with three minutes to go, Thierry Henry sent a tame header into Craig Gordon's gloves, the reaction of the crowd was as loud as it was for the goal itself. In the stands you could hear the murmurs: "You know, we could actually do this!"

Rangers Call Walter 'Home'

Four days after that magical Glasgow evening came defeat in the Ukraine. After the sheer exertion of the weekend's endeavours it was remarkable the players could take to the pitch, never mind taking on a team the calibre of Ukraine. That defeat could not dent the new-found optimism felt by all associated with the national team, as they ended 2006 as joint leaders of Group B.

The 2-0 loss to Ukraine was to prove to be Scotland's last match under Walter Smith. In January 2007 Rangers had hit crisis point. Already too far behind Celtic to be considered title rivals, out of the League and Scottish Cups, a change needed to be made. Unfortunately for the national team, the man turned to by Sir David Murray was the one the Tartan Army had most feared. Walter Smith had guided Rangers to nine league titles in a row in the 1990's, and after success with Scotland, he was chosen to lead Rangers for a second spell.

Replacing the man who had lifted Scotland 70 places further up the world rankings than when he arrived was not going to be an easy task.

Eck's the Boss

By the end of January 2007 Alex McLeish was appointed to succeed Walter Smith. On the whole this was a popular appointment, as 'Big Eck' was deemed to sport the same characteristics as his predecessor: strong leader, purveyor of spirit, good tactician, and a man who sets up his team to play to their strengths.

It was almost two months before McLeish was to select his first side, and it was one which bore a striking resemblance to Smith's team, in both shape and personnel. 'If it ain't broke don't fix it' was the motto as McLeish set about continuing the excellent start to Scotland's qualifying campaign.

A last-minute goal from Craig Beattie got the new boss off to a great start, and although defeat in Italy was to follow, all the signs were positive that the group would go to the wire. Before the 2006-07 season was over, Scotland were another three points better off, courtesy of a comfortable win in the Faroes.

Scotland were almost robbed of a fourth straight home win by what was deemed the treachery of Saulius Mikoliunas. When up 1-0 and apparently coasting to the victory, the Lithuanian winger deceived the referee into giving a penalty for a 'foul' by Darren Fletcher. The penalty was converted, but justice was done as two late goals gave Scotland a 3-1 victory, and Mikoliunas was given a two-match ban for his antics. With two-thirds of the qualification now completed Scotland were very much in contention, and the best was yet to come…

So Near…

The night of September 12 2007 will go down as one of the greatest ever nights for Scottish sport. Tens of thousands of Tartan Army foot-soldiers descended on the Parc de Princes - many joining a march to the ground from the Eiffel Tower - to see a wonder goal by James McFadden ensure a famous double over the French.

SCOTLAND

EURO RE-VISION

When Ukraine were beaten 3-1 at Hampden, it was not just the hardcore optimists that were backing Scotland. Bookmakers and pundits alike made Scotland favourites to qualify from Group B, quite remarkable in itself considering the position little over a year before. However, as most Scots will remember, the tag of favourites does not bode well for a country which has made its reputation from being the underdog. Like the World Cup in Argentina 1978, pride comes before a fall…

…and Yet so Far

Just fours days after the win over Ukraine at Hampden, came the trip to Georgia to play a team which had long-since lost any hope of qualifying for the Finals themselves. Fielding a team including a 16 year-old and two 17 year-olds, the Georgians played like a team with nothing to lose and took the lead 16 minutes into the match. Scotland did not have much in the way of chances, but then came what seemed to be the pivotal moment in the ultimately fruitless campaign.

German referee Knut Kircher denied what looked to be a clear-cut penalty in the 34th minute. Zurab Khizanishvili fouled McFadden in the box, but nothing was given. Football matches, and even whole tournaments, can turn in a split-second and in that moment this one appeared to turn away from Scotland. Would they have qualified had Mr Kircher given that penalty? Maybe not, but had it been given and scored, you would have fancied the Scots to have got something out the game.

After the 2-0 defeat in Tbilisi, qualifying for Euro 2008 was still in their own hands, but the men in navy blue knew the enormity of the task - beating the World Champions at home.

That task was made all the more difficult when Luca Toni gave Italy the lead in the opening minutes. A couple of slices of luck meant Scotland were level just after the hour. Firstly Antonio Di Natale had an effort ruled out incorrectly for offside then, for the equaliser, Barry Ferguson was offside when he turned home the rebound of a Lee McCulloch shot. It was Italy however who had the last laugh and last slice of fortune with just seconds to go. Alan Hutton was penalised in a decision that should have gone the other way. From the resultant free-kick, Christian Panucci rose highest to head past Craig Gordon and by doing so ended Scotland's hopes of qualification.

The Future's Bright

That might have been that for Euro 2008, but with the ranking boost this remarkable campaign had given Scotland, there must be a real chance of seeing them in a major finals for the first time in twelve years come South Africa 2010.

European Championship Games

Date	Opponents	Venue	Score	Scorers
02/09/2006	Faroe Islands	H	6-0	Fletcher, McFadden, Boyd 2, Miller, O'Connor
06/09/2006	Lithuania	A	1-2	Miceika, Dailly, Miller
07/10/2006	France	H	1-0	Caldwell
11/10/2006	Ukraine	A	2-0	Kucher, Shevchenko
24/03/2007	Georgia	H	2-1	Boyd, Beattie, Arveladze
28/03/2007	Italy	A	2-0	Toni 2
06/06/2007	Faroe Islands	A	0-2	Maloney, O'Connor
08/09/2007	Lithuania	H	3-1	Boyd, McManus, McFadden, Danilevicius
12/09/2007	France	A	0-1	McFadden
13/10/2007	Ukraine	H	3-1	Miller, McCulloch, McFadden, Shevchenko
17/10/2007	Georgia	A	2-0	Mchedlidze, Siradze
17/11/2007	Italy	H	1-2	Ferguson, Toni, Panucci

As Scotland manager, the expectations of five million people rest on your shoulders. Here, we look back at several managers who have made their own unique mark on the national team.

IAN McCOLL

As part of a strong Rangers defence, known as 'the iron curtain', Ian McColl won an impressive 13 trophies in the 1940's and 50's. The defender was also awarded 14 international caps for Scotland.

After he retired as a player in 1960, he soon became a manager. He took charge of Scotland between 1961 and 1965.

McColl had an extremely gifted squad of players during his time as manager. Players such as Denis Law, Frank McLintock and Dave MacKay all played for big clubs in England.

However, McColl's first game was humiliating. Scotland played England at Wembley in April 1961 and the English ran out winners by 9-3. Not a great start.

His next task was to qualify for the 1962 World Cup in Chile. Scotland won three of their four games, but failed to make it through. However, they bounced back under McColl, winning the British Championships in 1962 and 1963. Scotland won all three matches against Wales, Northern Ireland and England in the 1961-1962 championships and again a year later. In the 1962-63 championships, Scotland beat Northern Ireland 5-1, with Manchester United legend Denis Law scoring four times. In the final game against England in 1963, Rangers' Jim Baxter scored twice at Hampden to earn a 2-0 win.

1963 was a good year for Scotland. McColl also guided the Scots to some brilliant wins in friendly matches.

A year later, Scotland beat England for the third time in a row. Alan Gilzean scored the winner in a 1-0 win at Hampden.

McColl resigned in 1965 following a 0-0 draw at home to Spain.

JOCK STEIN

Here was a man who truly gave his life for football. Jock Stein, affectionately known as 'Big Jock', is one of the greatest managers in Scottish football history.

In the 1960's he managed Dunfermline, where he won the Scottish Cup, and Hibernian before moving to Celtic in 1965. While at Celtic, Stein master-minded an amazing nine Scottish league titles in a row. In 1967, Celtic won the European Cup, beating Inter Milan 2-1 in the final. Stein was the first British manager to win this trophy.

Stein managed Scotland twice. His first spell was in 1965 when Scotland were trying to qualify for the World Cup in 1966, held in England. Scotland did not qualify but managed a heroic 1-0 win against Italy at Hampden in November 1965 in front of over 100,000 fans.

His second spell in charge was between 1978 and 1985. After missing out on Euro '80, Stein turned his attention to qualification for the

World Cup. Scotland beat their main rivals in the group, Sweden, twice to make it to the finals, held in Spain. In the middle of the qualifiers, Scotland also beat the 'auld enemy' England 1-0 at Wembley in the British Championships of 1981.

At the finals, Scotland lost 4-1 to brilliant Brazil in their second game after hammering New Zealand 5-2, Scotland's biggest win in World Cup history. But, in the final game, Scotland could only draw with USSR and went home early once again.

Stein continued to manage Scotland for another three years but, in 1985, disaster struck. Scotland were playing Wales in a qualifier for the 1986 World Cup. At the end of the match, which ended 1-1, Stein had a heart attack and died. His death devastated the Scottish nation and the world of football.

He will never be forgotten and now has a stand named after him at Celtic Park.

MANAGING THE DREAM

WILLIE ORMOND

Willie Ormond enjoyed an excellent career in football, as both a player and a manager. In the 1950's he played for Hibernian. Ormond was part of Hibs' best-ever team. Hibs played with five forwards at the time, known as 'the famous five'. Ormond scored 193 goals for the Hibees and won six caps for Scotland.

His first job as manager was at St Johnstone. Here he took Saints into European competition for the first time in 1969. He was well respected in Scotland and in 1973 he was appointed as manager of the Scottish national team.

His first game was one to forget. Scotland lost 5-0 to England at Hampden. But, after a stunning win against Czechoslovakia, Scotland qualified for the 1974 World Cup in West Germany. Three weeks before the tournament, Ormond enjoyed some revenge against England with a 2-0 win.

Ormond went on to manage Scotland for 3 more years but resigned in 1977. Sadly, he died seven years later at the age of 57.

SIR ALEX FERGUSON

He may be more famous for his great success as a club manager but Sir Alex Ferguson did manage Scotland briefly between 1985 and 1986.

Fergie started his career as a manager in 1974 with East Stirling before moving to St Mirren and then Aberdeen. He worked miracles with the Dons, winning 10 trophies in eight years including the European Cup Winners' Cup in 1983.

When Jock Stein sadly died in 1985, Ferguson stepped in to take control of the national team for the late stages of the qualifiers for the World Cup. He continued to manage Aberdeen at the same time. After drawing his first game in charge in a friendly with East Germany, Ferguson was faced with a World Cup play-off against Australia. The first leg was at Hampden. It was a tense match but ended with a 2-0 win for the Scots. The return match was held in

Melbourne where a 0-0 draw was enough to see Scotland qualify for the finals in Mexico.

At the World Cup, Sir Alex was handed group matches against Denmark, West Germany and Uruguay. Denmark beat Scotland 1-0 in the opening match. Next up was West Germany, one of the best teams in the world. The Scots stunned the Germans, and the world, when they took the lead with a great goal from Gordon Strachan. But Rudi Voller soon equalised and Scotland went on to lose bravely by 2 goals to 1.

A 0-0 draw against Uruguay in their final game meant Scotland were out and Ferguson resigned soon after.

Fergie went on to manage Manchester United where he has won 10 Premier League titles, five FA Cups, two League Cups, two Champions Leagues and a Cup Winners' Cup.

ANDY ROXBURGH

Born in Glasgow in 1943, for most of his life Andy Roxburgh has been involved in football. As a player he made over 200 appearances for five clubs including Queen's Park and Partick Thistle before retiring in 1975. However, he is better known for his time as a manager.

Roxburgh managed Scotland at many levels. He guided the under 19's to victory in the 1982 European Under-19 Championships. He was admired for his work with young players and was rewarded by the SFA in July 1986 when he was given the job as Scotland manager.

Roxburgh enjoyed mixed success in charge of the national team. Under Roxburgh, Scotland failed to qualify for the European Championships of 1988. After this disappointment, he then made amends when the Scots made it through to the World Cup in 1990, famously knocking out France in the qualifiers.

Roxburgh's finest achievement as Scotland manager was qualifying for the European Championships in 1992, the first time Scotland had made it through to this tournament.

At Euro '92 Scotland were given a very hard group and lost their first two games against holders Holland and world champions Germany. Scotland won 3-0 in their last match against the CIS but did not qualify from the section.

Roxburgh's final campaign as manager was the qualifiers for the 1994 World Cup. Scotland only managed wins against Malta and Estonia and finished 4th in a group of six teams.

Roxburgh resigned as manager in September 1993.

Fabulous Facts About Scotland

TARTAN TRIVIA

- Scotland's first international match was played on a cricket pitch in Glasgow. West of Scotland's cricket ground in Partick staged a match between Scotland and England on November 30, 1872 that finished in a 0-0. It was the world's first international match.

- Scotland's first international goal was scored by Henry Renny-Tailyour (Royal Engineers) in a 4-2 defeat by England at the Kennington Oval in London in 1873.

- Scotland's first international win was against England in the annual international the following year. Goals from Frederick Anderson (Clydesdale) and William McKinnon (Queen's Park) gave them a 2-1 win at Hamilton Crescent.

- John McDougall (Vale of Leven) had the distinction of being the first Scotland player to score an international hat-trick. He managed it in a 7-2 demolition of England at the original Hampden Park in 1878.

- Wales also played annual matches against Scotland from 1876 but they did not score in their first four matches. Even when they managed to put the ball past the Scotland goalkeeper – George Gillespie of Rangers – Scotland still won the 1880 match 5-1.

- Queen's Park have the biggest representation in a Scotland team after providing all eleven players for that first international against England in 1872. Rangers provided seven for the 1900 international against Wales and Celtic had six in the Scotland team as recently as 1967 for a match against the USSR.

- Hugh Gallagher (Newcastle United) has scored more goals than any other Scotland player in a single match when he contributed five in a 7-3 win over Northern Ireland in Belfast in 1929.

- George Young (Rangers) has captained Scotland more times than any other player – 48 times in all.

- David Allan (Queen's Park) scored Scotland's 100th international goal. It came in an 8-1 rout of Wales in 1885 with Allan scoring the third of the eight goals that day.

- Mo Johnston – then playing for Nantes – scored Scotland's 1,000th international goal in a World Cup qualifier against Yugoslavia in 1988 at Hampden. The game finished 1-1.

- Kenny Dalglish is Scotland's most-capped player with 102 caps. He also shares the record for the number of goals scored for his country (30) with Denis Law.

- Scotland's biggest international win was 11-0 against Northern Ireland in Glasgow in 1901 with Alex McMahon (Celtic) and Robert Hamilton (Rangers) both scoring four goals.

- Scotland's record defeat was 7-0 against Uruguay at the 1954 World Cup finals in Switzerland. Tommy Docherty and Willie Ormond, who both went on to manage the national side, were both in the team.

- Ronnie Simpson (Celtic) was the oldest Scottish player to make his international debut when he won his first cap in the famous 1967 win over England at Wembley at the age of 36 years and 186 days.

- Scotland's most-capped goalkeeper Jim Leighton went 469 minutes without conceding a goal for Scotland from April 1987 to February 1988.

- Scotland's highest attendance for a home match is 149,415 against England at Hampden in April 1937. Scotland won 3-1.

- The biggest crowd to watch Scotland outside of Glasgow was 130,000 for a match against Brazil at the Maracana Stadium in Rio de Janeiro in 1972. Brazil won 1-0 thanks to an 80th-minute goal from Jairzinho.

- Andy Beattie was the first Scotland manager and was appointed in February 1954 but lasted only a few months. He had a second spell in charge five years later but then left because of club commitments with Nottingham Forest.

- John Lambie (Queen's Park) is the youngest player to have been capped by Scotland, making his debut at 17 years and 92 days against Northern Ireland in a 7-2 win in 1886. He was also captain of the team that day.

- Scotland's most prolific goalscorer is Hugh Gallagher (Airdrie and Newcastle United) who scored 23 goals in just 20 appearances.

TARTAN ARMY

The Best Supporters In The World.....

SCOTLAND

TARTAN ARMY TRIBUTE

28

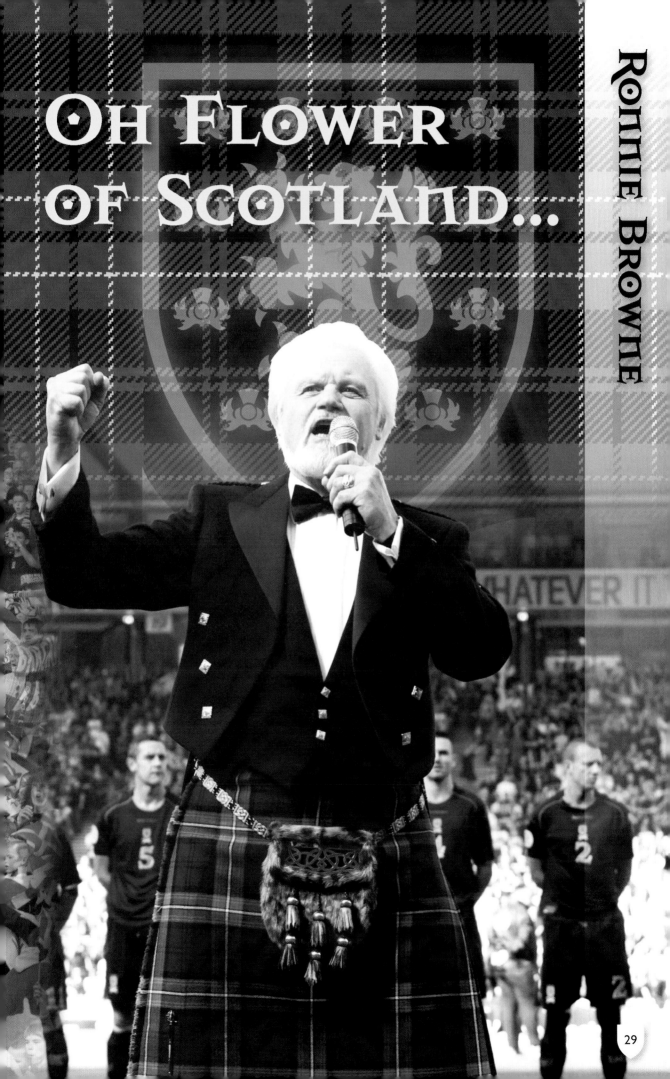

Oh Flower of Scotland...

Ronnie Browne

MAD on McFADDEN

James McFadden has scored some crucial and spectacular goals in a Scotland shirt and here we look at a few of his memorable efforts

Match: Scotland 3 Faroes 1
Dateline: September 6, 2003
Venue: Hampden Park, Glasgow

74 minutes: It's a must-win game and Scotland hold just a narrow lead against the Faroes in their European Championships qualifying match. Enter McFadden. There are just 16 minutes left when Neil McCann rolls the ball into the path of the new Everton striker and he makes no mistake from five yards to celebrate his first goal for his country.

Match: Scotland 1 Holland 0
Dateline: November 15, 2003
Venue: Hampden Park, Glasgow

22 minutes: Scotland are seeking a lead to take to Holland in this European Championships play-off match. Midway through the first half, McFadden's corner comes back out to him on the right. He does not launch it back into the penalty area as expected but plays a one-two with Darren Fletcher before shooting from a tight angle. The ball sails over the head of Edwin van der Sar with the aid of a deflection as Hampden erupts.

Match: Slovenia 0 Scotland 3
Dateline: October 12, 2005
Venue: Arena Petrol, Celje

47 minutes: Nigel Quashie starts the move when he feeds Darren Fletcher who, in turn, picks out McFadden. The striker produces a top-class finish as he lofts the ball over goalkeeper Samir Handanovic to give the Scots a 2-0 lead early in the second half in Celje. Unfortunately, it is too late for Scotland to qualify for the World Cup but the win does help their seeding for Euro 2008.

Match: Scotland 5 Bulgaria 1
Dateline: May 11, 2006
Venue: Kobe Wing Stadium, Kobe, Japan

69 minutes: McFadden, who had replaced two-goal Kris Boyd earlier, scores Scotland's third when he somehow manages to divert a near-post cross from Gary Teale away from goalkeeper Stoyan Kolev and into the far side of the net in spite of being closely guarded by a defender. It helps Scotland to an emphatic Kirin Cup win.

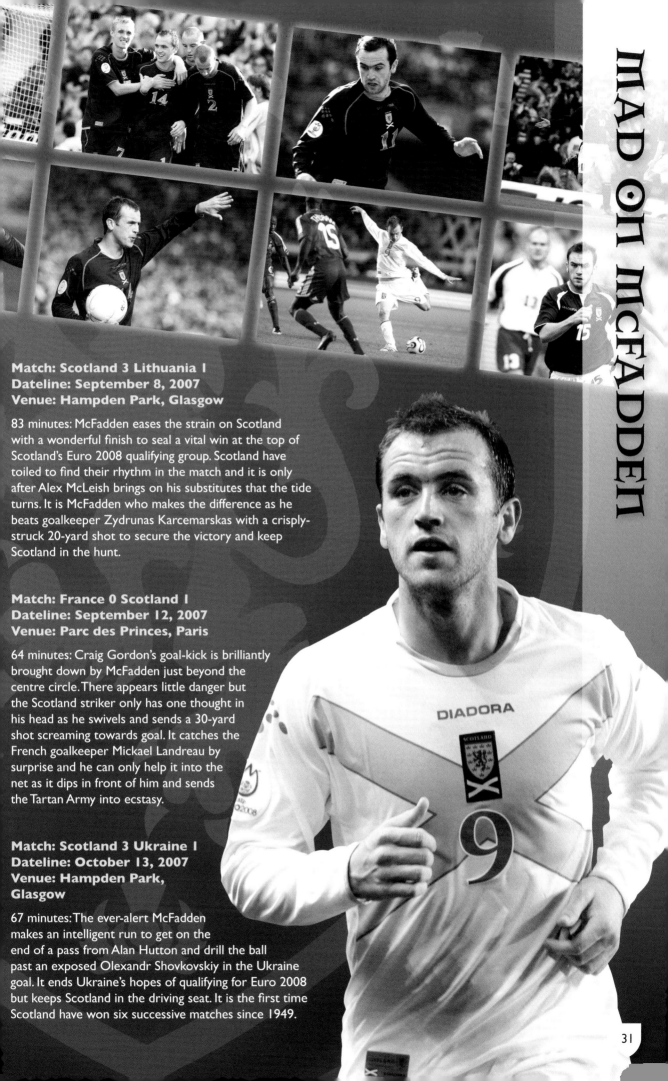

Match: Scotland 3 Lithuania 1
Dateline: September 8, 2007
Venue: Hampden Park, Glasgow

83 minutes: McFadden eases the strain on Scotland with a wonderful finish to seal a vital win at the top of Scotland's Euro 2008 qualifying group. Scotland have toiled to find their rhythm in the match and it is only after Alex McLeish brings on his substitutes that the tide turns. It is McFadden who makes the difference as he beats goalkeeper Zydrunas Karcemarskas with a crisply-struck 20-yard shot to secure the victory and keep Scotland in the hunt.

Match: France 0 Scotland 1
Dateline: September 12, 2007
Venue: Parc des Princes, Paris

64 minutes: Craig Gordon's goal-kick is brilliantly brought down by McFadden just beyond the centre circle. There appears little danger but the Scotland striker only has one thought in his head as he swivels and sends a 30-yard shot screaming towards goal. It catches the French goalkeeper Mickael Landreau by surprise and he can only help it into the net as it dips in front of him and sends the Tartan Army into ecstasy.

Match: Scotland 3 Ukraine 1
Dateline: October 13, 2007
Venue: Hampden Park, Glasgow

67 minutes: The ever-alert McFadden makes an intelligent run to get on the end of a pass from Alan Hutton and drill the ball past an exposed Olexandr Shovkovskiy in the Ukraine goal. It ends Ukraine's hopes of qualifying for Euro 2008 but keeps Scotland in the driving seat. It is the first time Scotland have won six successive matches since 1949.

Test your knowledge about Scotland.

Instant Recall

1   Who scored Scotland's goal in the 3-1 friendly defeat by the Czech Republic in May 2008?

2   Which Hearts' player gained his first cap for Scotland in the same match in Prague?

3   Who scored Scotland's first goal under George Burley?

4   Who captained Scotland in the first match in the George Burley era?

5   Only three players started and finished George Burley's first two matches in charge – against Croatia and the Czech Republic – who were they?

Euro 2008 Qualifying

6   Which players scored for Italy at Hampden to end Scotland's qualifying hopes?

7   Who scored Scotland's final goal of the qualifying campaign?

8   Who scored for Scotland in the 2-0 win in the Faroes?

9   Which player scored against Ukraine at Hampden but picked up a booking and missed the trip to face Georgia?

10   Who captained Scotland when they beat Lithuania at Hampden?

Friendly Fire

11   Who scored Scotland's goal when they beat Euro 2008 hosts Austria 1-0 in Vienna in May 2007?

12   Which country did Scotland beat in a friendly at Pittodrie in August 2007?

13   Who started in goal for Scotland in Vienna in May 2007?

14   Who scored Scotland's goal in the 3-1 defeat by Switzerland in March 2006?

15   Who scored Scotland's goal against USA at Hampden in the 1-1 draw in November 2005?

World Cup

16   Which country have Scotland faced four times in the final stages of the World Cup?

17   In what year did Scotland first compete in the World Cup finals?

18   Which player scored for Scotland in three successive World Cup finals?

19   Which African nation did Scotland face in the 1974 World Cup finals in Germany?

20   Who was the last manager to take Scotland to the World Cup finals?

Answers on Page 61

N	J	M	C	C	O	I	T	K	F	J
A	C	O	L	L	I	N	S	M	X	U
D	I	K	W	A	S	E	E	I	N	L
R	N	T	A	H	G	U	O	G	C	A
O	W	M	K	B	N	T	C	O	H	X
J	I	A	X	E	H	B	C	R	E	S
G	Y	W	L	G	N	G	M	A	N	T
E	H	C	I	O	O	U	G	M	D	Y
I	G	E	J	B	A	X	T	E	R	D
H	L	D	A	W	R	I	O	C	Y	W
B	T	M	U	K	J	O	R	D	X	O

Find these past Scotland players in the word-search (names can go diagonal, vertical, horizontal or backwards)

1.	LAW	6.	BAXTER
2.	JORDAN	7.	LEIGHTON
3.	MCCOIST	8.	GOUGH
4.	AITKEN	9.	GORAM
5.	HENDRY	10.	COLLINS

Solution on Page 61

Five of the Greatest Scotland Games – Ever!

What is Scotland's greatest game? The Wembley Wizards? The win over world champions England in 1967? Or beating France at the Parc des Princes in 2007? It is something the Tartan Army have debated over the years. Here are five of the best to rekindle the memories – all merit inclusion - but no doubt fans will have their own top five.

March 31, 1928 Home International Championship

England 1 Scotland 5

The "Wembley Wizards" set the benchmark for Scottish International teams to follow with a handsome victory over England at Wembley which was all the more celebrated as it was unexpected.

Scotland went into their final Home International fixture on the back of a 1-0 defeat by Northern Ireland at Hampden and a 2-2 draw with Wales in Wrexham. Expectations were not high as the international selectors had left out Jimmy McGrory and Bob McPhail in a surprise move but when the teams took the field, there was optimism that Scotland could pull off a shock in the wet conditions.

England hit the post early on but Scotland hit back immediately and Alex Jackson headed them in front

from an Alan Morton cross. It was the signal for Scotland to take control. England struggled to cope with the Scotland wingers Jackson and Morton and Alex James and Hughie Gallacher also contributed to a thrilling all-round display. James scored the second before half-time with a well-struck left-foot shot.

Scotland continued to dominate in the second half and, after James had struck the post with a volley, Jackson added the third from another Morton cross.

James made it 4-0 after being set up by Gallacher and England had no answers to the rampant Scots. Jackson completed his hat-trick with five minutes left after Morton had again set him up and the visiting fans could hardly believe what they were seeing.

There was a late consolation for England when Robert Kelly scored in the final minutes but it did not detract from Scotland's day.

Unfortunately, the "Wembley Wizards" would never play together as a team again and even such a result could not help the Scots finishing higher than third in the Home International table.

April 15, 1967 Home International Championship/ European Championships qualifier

England 2 Scotland 3

England – under Alf Ramsay – had won the World Cup just nine months beforehand on the same Wembley turf but Scotland gatecrashed the party by handing the world champions their first defeat since that famous win over West Germany.

Ramsay had named 10 of the 11 that had played in the final and the only change – Jimmy Greaves for Roger Hunt – hardly weakened their cause. Scotland handed

a debut to 36 year-old Celtic goalkeeper Ronnie Simpson and also to 20 year-old Sheffield Wednesday forward Jim McCalliog and few gave them hope of an upset in the Home International match that also doubled as a European Championships qualifier.

Denis Law opened the scoring after 27 minutes after Willie Wallace's initial shot had been saved by Gordon Banks. England had been unbeaten in 19 internationals but Scotland controlled most of the game and Bobby Lennox shot the second goal from the edge of the box after 78 minutes.

It set up a frantic finish with Jack Charlton

pulling a goal back for England after a fine exchange between Alan Ball and Greaves and then Banks producing a breathtaking one-handed save to keep out a lob by Denis Law.

McCalliog marked his debut with a well-taken goal to make it 3-1 with just three minutes left but, a minute later, Geoff Hurst headed in a Bobby Charlton cross to cut Scotland's lead back to one again. But the Scots held out for a famous victory in a match that will be remembered for Jim Baxter's ball-juggling to torment the English as Scotland dominated for long spells.

Ultimately, however, it was England who were to qualify for the later stages of the European Championships the following year after Scotland lost 1-0 to Northern Ireland in Belfast in the October and could only draw 1-1 with England at Hampden the following February.

September 26, 1973
World Cup qualifier

Scotland 2 Czechoslovakia 1

Scotland hadn't qualified for a World Cup finals since 1958 but there was genuine hope that this team could get the win they needed to qualify for West Germany the following year. Scotland had beaten Denmark – the only other team in the three-nation group – home and away and the door to qualification had opened up after Czechoslovakia dropped a point to the Danes.

A hundred thousand fans made it an intimidating atmosphere for the Czechs at Hampden but this was a highly-rated team which was to form the foundations of the one that won the European Championships less than three years later.

Denis Law won his 50th cap for Scotland and Coventry City's Tommy

Hutchison his first along with Celtic's elegant half-back George Connelly.

The tension was evident at Hampden that night after Scotland had been in similar positions before only to lose out when opportunity knocked. Fears seemed to be justified after 33 minutes when Zdenek Nehoda caught out Ally Hunter with a speculative shot which the Scotland goalkeeper seemed to lose in flight.

Hampden was stunned but they had only seven minutes to wait for an equaliser when centre-half Jim Holton rose at a corner to head the ball into the net with just five minutes of the first half remaining.

Scotland knew that the dream was still there and they laid siege to the Czech goal in the second half. But, as the minutes ticked by, it looked as if the well-organised Czech team would hold on for a point. Kenny Dalglish went off to be replaced by young Leeds United striker Joe Jordan, who was winning his fourth cap.

It was Jordan who proved the match-winner with just 15 minutes left when Willie Morgan played in a cross and he stooped to head the ball beyond Ivo Viktor, the celebrated Czech goalkeeper.

June 11, 1978 World Cup finals, Argentina

Holland 2 Scotland 3

Scotland went into the 1978 World Cup finals in Argentina with high hopes as Britain's only representatives and the infectious enthusiasm of manager Ally MacLeod.

Unfortunately, it all went horribly wrong with a 3-1 opening defeat by Peru in their group and an insipid 1-1 draw with Iran. It left Scotland needing to beat Holland – World Cup finalists four years earlier – by three goals to progress. It was surely mission impossible in Mendoza.

But Scotland finally produced a performance and Bruce Rioch headed against the crossbar and Kenny Dalglish had a "goal" disallowed in the first half-hour.

The task became even more difficult after 34 minutes when Robbie Rensenbrink put the Dutch ahead from the penalty spot, meaning Scotland had to somehow find four goals in response.

Dalglish supplied one of them a minute from half-time when he hooked the ball over Jan Jongbloed to at least put Scotland in at the interval on level terms. It was an effort the

Scottish fans seemed to appreciate after the anti-climax of the opening two matches.

Archie Gemmill then put Scotland ahead from the penalty spot early in the second half to suggest at least there might be a victory of some sorts against one of the favourites for the trophy. Remarkably, Gemmill then conjured up what many rate as the greatest goal in Scotland's history when he gathered the ball outside the area and then waltzed through the Dutch defence before lofting it over Jongbloed. At 3-1, there were those who dared to dream.

Those dreams lasted barely three minutes when Jonny Rep beat Alan Rough with a long-range effort to finally crush Scotland's false hopes. Holland were not beaten again until they lost in the final to Argentina.

September 12, 2007 European Championship qualifier

France 0 Scotland 1

Whatever James McFadden achieves in his career, he will struggle to match this September night in Paris.

Scotland's seemingly hopeless task of reaching Euro 2008 would surely be confirmed at the Parc Des Princes. The French were out for revenge after losing at Hampden earlier in the group.

Since that match, Walter Smith had vacated the manager's chair and Alex McLeish had taken over and he set out his tactics to frustrate the French and defend in depth. France had most of the possession but Scotland kept Craig Gordon well protected for the most part. Florent Malouda and Franck Ribery threatened on more than one occasion in the first half but Scotland defended diligently and Gordon would have expected a busier night.

With the scores locked at 0-0 at half-time, there was still hope that Scotland could hold on for an unlikely point. McFadden's ambitions proved even wilder as he killed a long clearance from Gordon after 65 minutes and ran at the French before unleashing a stunning 35-yard shot which French goalkeeper Mickael Landreau could only help into the net.

The giant scoreboard confirmed that Scotland had taken the lead against mighty France much to the disbelief of the Tartan Army.

It would prove a tense final 25 minutes as Scotland battled to hold on to their lead. Gordon saved well from Ribery and Nicolas Anelka in the closing stages but somehow McLeish's side held on for arguably the greatest result in their history.

Scotland still had Ukraine, Georgia and Italy to face in the group but, with two of those at home, hopes were still high that Scotland could qualify out of a group that included the two teams that contested the last World Cup final.

However, it was not to be as Scotland lost in Georgia and then were beaten by Italy in their final match at Hampden to miss out on qualification.

Lion CUBS

George Burley has shown he is prepared to give youth its fling. We look at some of the young players coming through who will play a part in Scotland bidding to reach South Africa 2010.

STEVEN FLETCHER

Born in Shrewsbury, Steven Fletcher lived in Hamilton as a youngster and was recruited by Hibernian at the age of 13 after being spotted by then youth coach John Park.

It was obvious from an early age that he had an eye for goal and he was given his chance under Tony Mowbray when Garry O'Connor and Derek Riordan left for pastures new.

Many felt Hibs would struggle to fill the void left by those two but Fletcher stepped up to the plate and quickly became a favourite with the Easter Road fans.

He assured himself a place in the club's folklore when he scored two goals in the team's 5-1 win over Kilmarnock in the CIS League Cup final in 2007 under John Collins.

Fletcher was already making his mark at international level and was top scorer for the Scotland Under-19 team that went on to reach the final of the European Championships in Poland. The striker missed the final against Spain due to suspension, which saw the Scots go down 2-1.

But George Burley awarded him his first full cap against Croatia in the 1-1 draw in March 2008 when he laid on the Scotland goal for Kenny Miller before his involvement was curtailed due to injury.

SCOTLAND

DAVID CLARKSON

David Clarkson took less than 15 minutes to make his mark in a Scotland shirt. Called up for Scotland's friendly match against the Czech Republic in Prague, he came on as a late substitute for Gavin Rae.

Trailing 2-0, he brilliantly controlled a cross on the edge of the six-yard box before swivelling to send a stunning left-foot shot beyond one of the best goalkeepers in the world, Petr Cech.

It was a thrilling start to the Motherwell striker's international career but would have come as no surprise to the legions of Fir Park fans who have seen him score regularly in the claret-and-amber.

Born in Bellshill, he is a product of the Motherwell youth system which has produced the likes of James McFadden and Stephen Pearson in recent years.

He made his debut at the end of season 2001-02 in a match against Kilmarnock when he was only 16 and has gone on to make over 200 appearances for Motherwell.

In 2007-08, Clarkson enjoyed his best season in a Motherwell shirt as he banged in 13 goals and he will want to build on that form to convince George Burley that he cannot be ignored for international selection.

CHRISTOPHE BERRA

A few eyebrows were raised when Christophe Berra was handed the captain's armband at Hearts at the age of 22 but it was no surprise to insiders at the club.

The central defender learned his trade at Tynecastle under Steven Pressley and Andy Webster and when both departed, he had to grow up quickly.

His pace and ability to read the game at the back had him being groomed for the international game at an early age and George Burley duly recognised his potential by awarding him his first cap in the international against the Czech Republic in Prague.

Berra only came on for the final couple of minutes but at least he had the chance to taste international football and he is likely to play a more significant role in the years ahead.

Whoever he plays alongside at the back, he looks at ease and his dependability and willingness to go in where it hurts has made him a favourite with the Hearts' fans.

He played for Scotland right through from youth level to the Under-21s before making his full debut, he was also eligible to play for France through parentage.

Lion CUBS

JAMES MORRISON

Morrison represented England at Under-20 level, but qualifies to compete for Scotland due to his grandparents.

Born in Darlington, James was a product of Middlesbrough's famous youth system and he was an integral part of the team that won the FA Youth Cup. It wasn't long before he made his first-team debut for the club – in an FA Cup tie against Notts County at the age of 17.

He went on to play in the 2006 UEFA Cup final against Seville in Eindhoven and actually has the distinction of scoring the club's first-ever European goal.

He played 98 games for Middlesbrough, scoring eight goals, before moving to West Brom in a £1.5 million deal in 2007.

He helped the club secure promotion to the Premier League and also reach the semi-finals of the FA Cup under Tony Mowbray.

The talented midfield player did not go unnoticed by George Burley and he gave him a starting berth in the friendly international against the Czech Republic in Prague when he gave a solid display.

Always looking to go forward and try the unexpected, he could become a key player in the Scotland midfield in the years ahead.

ROSS McCORMACK

Another who made his international debut in Scotland's friendly with the Czech Republic in Prague in May 2008.

This time, he only had eight minutes to prove himself after replacing Barry Robson but it was a reward for his consistent play at club level for Motherwell where he helped the team secure a UEFA Cup berth.

Working under Mark McGhee has given the player a new lease of life and he was one of the big successes for the Fir Park side in 2007-08.

He started his career at Rangers where he famously scored a late equalising goal against FC Porto in Portugal after coming off the bench to keep Rangers' European hopes alive.

But he was thought surplus to requirements at Ibrox in the brief Paul Le Guen era and he was farmed out on loan to Doncaster Rovers.

He joined Motherwell in 2006 but his first season at the club was blighted by injury and illness and it was not until the 2007-08 season that Fir Park fans saw the best of him.

He notched 11 goals for the club as they secured third place but also created a number of goals for his team-mates with his direct running and willingness to take players on.

There was a time when Scottish goalkeepers were the butt of jokes. That has changed in recent years and here we look back on a few players who have served their country with distinction as the last line of defence.

TOMMY YOUNGER

Born and brought up in Edinburgh, Tommy Younger signed for Hibernian at an early age and went on to win two Scottish League titles with the Easter Road club in 1951 and 1952.

A dependable goalkeeper and terrific shot-stopper it was not long before his reputation grew and he was lured to Liverpool in a £9,000 deal in 1956. During his first season, he immediately established himself as the number one at Anfield and played in 43 of the 45 matches for the club that season.

A back injury led to him returning to Scotland for a brief spell as player-manager at Falkirk but, having recovered from the injury, he returned south and had spells at Stoke City and Leeds United before retiring.

He won his first cap for Scotland in a 3-0 friendly win over Portugal at Hampden in May 1955 and played in the 1958 World Cup finals in Sweden where he was goalkeeper in two of the three matches, against Yugoslavia and Paraguay.

The Paraguay match – his 24th cap – proved to be his final match for Scotland after three years as the national number one.

He stayed in the game as an administrator and was president of the Scottish Football Association before he died in 1984.

ALAN ROUGH

Alan Rough is Scotland's second most-capped goalkeeper behind Jim Leighton in spite of the fact that he spent much of his career with Partick Thistle, a club that did not compete for the major honours in the Scottish game.

Some argue that the reason he was such an accomplished shot-stopper was down to the fact he had so much practice at Partick, where he made over 600 appearances. The highlight of his time with the club was undoubtedly when he played in the 1971 League Cup final against Celtic when Thistle produced one of the huge upsets of the Scottish game, winning 4-1.

SAVING GRACE

Hibernian signed him in 1982 and he had six happy years at Easter Road before trying his luck across the pond and signing for Orlando Lions. He also had spells at Celtic, Hamilton Academical and Ayr United.

Rough made his Scotland debut in April 1976 in a 1-0 win over Switzerland at Hampden when Tommy Craig, Alex MacDonald, Frank Gray and Willie Pettigrew also made their first appearances.

He went on to play for Scotland in the World Cup finals in 1974 in Germany and 1978 in Argentina. He won his 53rd and final cap in the Rous Cup match against England at Wembley in 1986 where Scotland lost 2-1.

JIM LEIGHTON

Only Kenny Dalglish has won more Scotland caps than Jim Leighton. The former Aberdeen, Manchester United and Hibernian goalkeeper amassed 91 caps in a 16-year span from 1982-98.

He went to the 1982 World Cup in Spain as an understudy to Alan Rough but did not play. He was given his Scotland debut in October 1982 in a European Championships qualifier against East Germany at Hampden where he kept a clean sheet in a 2-0 win.

Leighton went on to become a permanent fixture in the Scotland team and played in three World Cups – in 1986, 1990 and 1998.

At club level, after playing for Alex Ferguson's successful Aberdeen team of the 1980s which won the European Cup-Winners' Cup, he followed the manager to Manchester United. But he

suffered a loss of form during his second season and was dropped for the 2000 FA Cup final replay at Crystal Palace and returned to Scotland to play, firstly for Dundee, and then for Hibs where his international career was rekindled after more than three years out of the reckoning.

After losing his place to Andy Goram, he returned for a World Cup qualifier in Malta and he again kept a clean sheet in a 2-0 win. He played for Scotland in the World Cup finals in France in 1998 but later that year announced his retirement from international football at the age of 40.

ANDY GORAM

Born in Bury, Lancashire, Goram spent the first seven years of his career at Oldham Athletic before Alex Miller signed him for Hibernian in 1987. He was keen to sign for the Edinburgh club, where his father, Lew, also played.

Goram played a big part in Hibs' revival under Miller and Rangers paid £1 million for his services in 1991. He became a firm favourite with the Ibrox fans and helped the team to the brink of the European Cup final in 1992-93 under Walter Smith. In 2001, he was voted the greatest goalkeeper in the club's history by Rangers' fans.

He won his first Scotland cap when he came on as a substitute for Jim Leighton in a 0-0 draw in a friendly against East Germany in October 1985 and played in friendly matches against Romania and Holland in the build-up to the 1986 World Cup finals in Mexico (keeping a clean sheet in both) but Alex Ferguson went with Leighton for the three matches in the finals.

He was to vie with Leighton for the international goalkeeping jersey over the coming years and it was not until after the 1990 World Cup that he was given an extended run by Andy Roxburgh, going on to win 43 international caps.

An all-rounder, Goram also represented Scotland at cricket while he was playing for Hibs.

CRAIG GORDON

A product of Hearts' youth academy, Craig Gordon has established himself as Scotland's undisputed number one in spite of his youth. Given his international debut by Berti Vogts in a 4-1 win over Trinidad & Tobago in May 2004, he has never let his country down.

After making his Hearts' debut in a 1-1 draw with Livingston in October 2002, he went on to displace Tepi Moilanen as the regular first-choice at Tynecastle. His reflex saves became a feature of his game at club level and it was no surprise that he earned his international call-up.

He helped the club finish second in the Premier League in 2005-06 where they qualified for the Champions' League and also won a Scottish Cup medal as Hearts beat Gretna in a penalty shoot-out,

Gordon making a crucial save from Derek Townsley.

Voted Scotland's Footballer of the Year in 2006 – the first Hearts player for 20 years to take the award – he was later named captain of the team. Sunderland signed him in a £9 million deal in August 2007, making him the UK's most expensive goalkeeper.

He excelled in Scotland's two victories over France in Euro 2008 qualifying, and has won himself admirers all over the world and, before his move to Sunderland, was linked to some of the biggest clubs in Europe.

Twenty questions for: Barry Ferguson, Alan Hutton, Darren Fletcher, Scott Brown and Stephen McManus.

Barry Ferguson

1 Age started playing?   8

2 School/boys' club team? Mill United Boys Club

3 Favourite food? Pasta

4 Favourite TV programme? The F Word or Ramsay's Kitchen Nightmares

5 Favourite film? Shawshank Redemption

6 Favourite singer/band? The Stone Roses

7 Sporting hero? Roger Federer or Tiger Woods

8 First game you went to see? Hamilton Accies

9 Earliest Scotland memory? 1st team debut in Lithuania

10 Favourite Scotland match? England v Scotland at Wembley in 1999

11 Favourite Scotland goal? Against Italy in Euro 2008

12 Best footballer ever? Maradona

13 Biggest influence on career? Dad and brother

14 Most difficult opponent? Connor and Kyle Ferguson

15 Favourite stadium? Ibrox

16 Proudest moment? Being made captain of Rangers and captain of Scotland

17 Tip for a young player?   Devotion to football

18 Ambitions in football? To lead Scotland to the World Cup in 2010

19 Hobbies outside football? Golf

20 If you weren't a footballer, what would you be doing? Working as a roofer with my Dad

Alan Hutton

1 Age started playing? 5

2 School/boys' club team? Kingsmead Boys' Club

3 Favourite food? Lasagne

4 Favourite TV programme? Eastenders

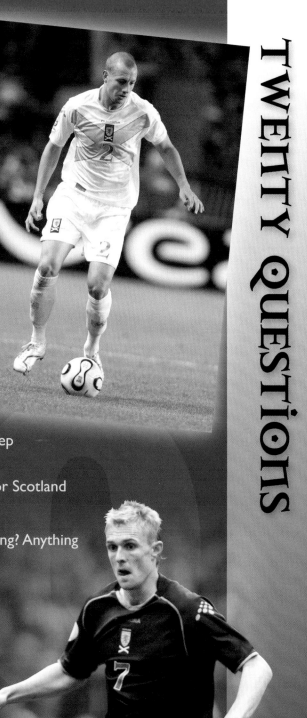

5   Favourite film? Scarface

6   Favourite singer/band? L'il Wayne

7   Sporting hero? Brian Laudrup

8   First game you went to see? Rangers v Aberdeen

9   Earliest Scotland memory? '94 World Cup

10   Favourite Scotland match? 1st competitive match against Lithuania

11   Favourite Scotland goal? McFadden's goal in Paris

12   Best footballer ever? Pele

13   Biggest influence on career? Dad

14   Most difficult opponent? Ronaldo

15   Favourite stadium? Nou Camp

16   Proudest moment? Birth of my two sons

17   Tip for a young player? Work hard, stick in and keep going no matter how many knocks you take

18   Ambitions in football? To play in the World Cup for Scotland

19   Hobbies outside football? Golf

20   If you weren't a footballer, what would you be doing? Anything else involving football

Darren Fletcher

1   Age started playing? 5

2   School/boys' club team? Langlaw Boys' Club

3   Favourite food? Pizza and chips

4   Favourite TV programme? Soccer AM

5   Favourite film? Any Given Sunday

6   Favourite singer/band? Jay Z

7   Sporting hero? Fernando Redondo

8   First game you went to see? Celtic v Hibs

9   Earliest Scotland memory? Murdo McLeod being knocked out in 1990 World Cup against Brazil

10   Favourite Scotland match? Beating France at Hampden in Euro 2008 Qualifier

11   Favourite Scotland goal? The 1st goal against Lithuania in Euro 2008 Qualifier

12   Best footballer ever? Zidane

13 Biggest influence on career? Dad

14 Most difficult opponent? Paul Scholes

15 Favourite stadium? The old Highbury

16 Proudest moment? Captaining Scotland in Estonia

17 Tip for a young player? Keep practising, always believe in yourself

18 Ambitions in football? To represent Scotland in a major tournament finals

19 Hobbies outside football? Poker, golf, the twins

20 If you weren't a footballer, what would you be doing? Coaching or PE teaching

Scott Brown

1 Age started playing? 8

2 School/boys' club team? Beith Centre

3 Favourite food? Pasta

4 Favourite TV programme? Friends

5 Favourite film? Braveheart

6 Favourite singer/band? Oasis

7 Sporting hero? Tiger Woods

8 First game you went to see? Hibs v Aberdeen

9 Earliest Scotland memory? Scotland v Brazil in France '98

10 Favourite Scotland match? France v Scotland in Paris in Euro 2008 Qualifying Campaign

11 Favourite Scotland goal? McFadden's goal in Paris

12 Best footballer ever? Maradona

13 Biggest influence on career? Tony Mowbray

14 Most difficult opponent? Kevin Thomson

15 Favourite stadium? Nou Camp

16 Proudest moment? Winning the league title with Celtic

17 Tip for a young player? Stick in and work hard

18 Ambitions in football? To play in the English Premiership and to play in the World Cup Finals with Scotland

19 Hobbies outside football? Golf

20 If you weren't a footballer, what would you be doing? Bin man

Stephen McManus

1 Age started playing? 4

2 School/boys' club team? St John the Baptist Primary, Holy Cross High School

3 Favourite food? Italian

4 Favourite TV programme? 24

5 Favourite film? A Bronx Tale

6 Favourite singer/band? Oasis, Snow Patrol, Coldplay

7 Sporting hero? Eric Cantona

8 First game you went to see? Celtic v Dundee Utd in 1986 or 1987

9 Earliest Scotland memory? Italia '90

10 Favourite Scotland match? Beating France Away 1-0

11 Favourite Scotland goal? Archie Gemmill against Holland

12 Best footballer ever? Maradona

13 Biggest influence on career? Dad

14 Most difficult opponent? Kaka

15 Favourite stadium? Celtic Park

16 Proudest moment? Being made captain of Celtic and also the chance to captain my country

17 Tip for a young player? Always believe in yourself

18 Ambitions in football? To win as many trophies as I can

19 Hobbies outside football? Golf

20 If you weren't a footballer, what would you be doing? Fireman

SCOTLAND

As Scotland looks towards South Africa 2010, we look back on the performances at previous World Cup finals.

Switzerland 1954

Austria 1 Scotland 0

Scotland team: Martin; Cunningham, Aird, Docherty, Davidson, Cowie, Mackenzie, Fernie, Mochan, Brown, Ormond.

Scotland made their debut in the finals against the highly-rated Austrians and gave a good account of themselves before losing out narrowly.

Austria scored the only goal of the game after 32 minutes when Erich Probst netted after good work from Alfred Korner.

Uruguay 7 Scotland 0

Scotland team: Martin; Cunningham, Aird, Docherty, Davidson, Cowie, Mackenzie, Fernie, Mochan, Brown, Ormond.

Scotland manager Andy Beattie resigned after the loss to Austria leaving Scotland to face an even bigger task against the reigning world champions.

Uruguay led 2-0 at half-time and any hopes of a comeback were dashed three minutes into the second half when Borges netted his second goal.

Julio Cesar Abbadie made it 4-0 before Borges completed his hat-trick after 58 minutes. Late goals from Miguez and Abbadie completed the rout and John Mackenzie missed a late chance for a consolation when he shot feebly from just a few yards out.

Sweden 1958

Scotland 1 Yugoslavia 1

Scotland team: Younger; Caldow, Hewie, Turnbull, Evans, Cowie, Leggat, Murray, Mudie, Collins, Imlach.

Aleksandar Petakovic stunned Scotland with a goal after only six minutes but the Scots hit back to take a point.

Vladimir Beara – the Yugoslav goalkeeper – did not look comfortable with crosses and Scotland took advantage when Jimmy Murray headed in a cross from Eddie Turnbull two minutes into the second half.

Paraguay 3 Scotland 2

Scotland team: Younger; Parker, Caldow, Turnbull, Evans, Cowie, Leggat, Collins, Mudie, Robertson, Fernie.

An early mistake from Alex Parker led to Paraguay's opening goal from Juan Bautista Aguero but Scotland equalised after 32 minutes when Jackie Mudie scored after Bobby Collins and Graham Leggat had combined to set up the chance.

Jose Parodi made it 3-1 after 74 minutes after Tommy Younger had dropped the ball. Collins scored from distance – the 500th goal of the World Cup finals.

France 2 Scotland 1

Scotland team: Brown; Caldow, Hewie, Turnbull, Evans, Mackay, Collins, Murray, Mudie, Baird, Imlach.

Scotland made changes for their final match and Bill Brown made his debut in goal. Kopa gave France the lead midway through the first half and a minute later John Hewie missed a penalty for Scotland when his effort struck the post.

Just Fontaine proved the difference. After laying on Kopa's goal, he scored the second on the stroke of half-time and also hit the crossbar twice.

Sammy Baird pulled a goal back midway through the second half but again the Scots fell short.

West Germany 1974

Scotland 2 Zaire 0

Scotland team: Harvey; Jardine, McGrain, Hay, Holton, Blackley, Dalglish (Hutchison 75), Bremner, Jordan, Law, Lorimer.

After a 16-year wait, Scotland faced a Zaire team competing in the finals for the first time. Peter Lorimer gave Scotland a 26th-minute lead with a sizzling volley after Joe Jordan had headed the ball into his path.

Jordan headed the second eight minutes later from a Billy Bremner free-kick but the Zaire goalkeeper Kazadi Mwamba was badly at fault.

Scotland failed to build on the lead in the second half and it was ultimately to prove costly in the group.

Brazil 0 Scotland 0

Scotland team: Harvey; Jardine, McGrain, Hay, Holton, Buchan, Morgan, Bremner, Dalglish, Jordan, Lorimer.

Willie Ormond made two changes for the match against the world champions with Martin Buchan and Willie Morgan coming in.

It was a game of few chances. Leivinha hit the crossbar for Brazil early on and Billy Bremner was just inches off target at the other end.

Davie Hay also came close with a long-range effort and Scotland fully deserved their draw to keep alive their hopes of qualifying for the later stages.

Scotland 1 Yugoslavia 1

Scotland team: Harvey; Jardine, McGrain, Hay, Holton, Buchan, Morgan, Bremner, Dalglish (Hutchison 65), Jordan, Lorimer.

Scotland needed a win to qualify or for Zaire to run Brazil close. Neither happened. Both teams kept it tight and Scotland's task was made more difficult when the Yugoslav substitute Stanislav Karasi headed his side into the lead with nine minutes left. Joe Jordan's equaliser came too late as Brazil won 3-0 so Scotland became the first team to exit the World Cup without losing a game.

Argentina 1978

Peru 3 Scotland 1

Scotland team: Rough; Kennedy, Buchan, Rioch (Gemmill 70), Burns, Forsyth, Dalglish, Hartford, Jordan, Masson (Macari 70), Johnston.

Scotland went to Argentina with high hopes but were brought down to earth in their first game.

Joe Jordan gave Scotland the lead after 19 minutes when a Bruce Rioch shot had been pushed out by goalkeeper Ramon Quiroga. Cesar Cueto equalised before half-time and Teofilo Cubillas struck two second-half goals, one direct from a free-kick.

Don Masson saw a second-half penalty saved by Quiroga as Scotland saw their last chance of salvaging things disappear.

Iran 1 Scotland 1

Scotland team: Rough; Jardine, Donachie, Hartford, Burns, Buchan (Forsyth 57), Macari, Gemmill, Dalglish (Harper 73), Jordan, Robertson.

Fewer than 8,000 fans turned out in Cordoba as Scotland under-achieved again. But Scotland were gifted a lead two minutes from half-time when Andranik Eskandarian put through his own goal under pressure from Joe Jordan.

Iran equalised after an hour when Iraj Danaifar beat Alan Rough at his near post with a low shot to give them an unexpected draw.

Scotland 3 Holland 2

Scotland team: Rough; Kennedy, Donachie, Rioch, Forsyth, Buchan, Gemmill, Hartford, Jordan, Souness, Dalglish.

Scotland needed to win by three goals to qualify and a 34th minute penalty from Rep Rensenbrink made it look like mission impossible.

But the Scots hit back and Dalglish equalised before half-time and Archie Gemmill made it 2-1 from the penalty spot after Graeme Souness had been fouled.

Gemmill then showed his individual brilliance to put Scotland 3-1 ahead with arguably the most famous Scottish goal of all time.

But Johnny Rep ended the dream with a long-range shot after 71 minutes as Scotland went out of the competition on goal difference.

Spain 1982

Scotland 5 New Zealand 2

Scotland team: Rough; McGrain, Gray, Wark, Evans, Hansen, Strachan, Souness, Brazil (Archibald 53), Dalglish (Narey 83), Robertson.

Scotland had a comfortable opening win in Malago but it was not without its anxiety. John Wark headed two goals after Kenny Dalglish had squeezed home the opening goal to give Scotland a 3-0 half-time lead.

But New Zealand came back in the second half and captain Steve Sumner pulled a goal back before Steve Wooddin made it 3-2.

John Robertson eased concern with a 73rd-minute free-kick before Steve Archibald headed in to restore Scotland's three-goal advantage.

SPAIN 82

S.F.A. © 1981

SCOTLAND & THE WORLD CUP

Brazil 4 Scotland 1

Scotland team: Rough; Narey, Gray, Wark, Miller, Hansen, Strachan (Dalglish 65), Souness, Archibald, Hartford (McLeish 69), Robertson.

This was a football festival in Brazil with David Narey giving Scotland a shock 18th-minute lead with his famous "toe-poke" after John Wark had headed down a Graeme Souness pass.

But then the Brazilians turned on the style. Zico equalised with a stunning free-kick before half-time and Oscar headed the second at the near post four minutes into the second half.

Eder made it 3-1 with an exquisite chip over Alan Rough and Falcao completed the scoring three minutes from time with a shot that went in off the post.

USSR 2 Scotland 2

Scotland team: Rough; Narey, Gray, Wark, Miller, Hansen, Strachan (McGrain 71), Souness, Archibald, Jordan (Brazil 71), Robertson.

Scotland needed a win to qualify and the recalled Joe Jordan gave hope with an early goal from a David Narey pass.

The USSR equalised after an hour when Aleksandr Chivadze scored and Ramaz Shengalia made it 2-1 after 84 minutes when Willie Miller and Alan Hansen collided going for the same ball.

Graeme Souness equalised with three minutes left but it was not enough as, for the third successive time, Scotland went out on goal difference.

Mexico 1986

Denmark 1 Scotland 0

Scotland team: Leighton; Gough, Malpas, Nicol, Aitken, McLeish, Miller, Souness, Strachan (Bannon 75), Nicholas, Sturrock (McAvennie 61).

Alex Ferguson was in charge for the latest World Cup campaign but Scotland came up against one of the best teams in Denmark's history.

In a tight encounter, the only goal came after 57 minutes when Preben Elkjaer picked up a loose ball that had come off Willie Miller to beat Jim Leighton.

Scotland tried to get back but Denmark were well organised at the back and stifled their threat.

West Germany 2 Scotland 1

Scotland team: Leighton; Gough, Nicol (McAvennie 60), Aitken, Malpas, Miller, Narey, Souness, Strachan, Bannon (Cooper 74), Archibald.

After their opening defeat, Scotland needed something against the star-studded Germans and Gordon Strachan provided them with the perfect opportunity when he scored a well-taken goal after 17 minutes.

But Germany had too many weapons and Rudi Voller equalised five minutes later after being set up by Klaus Allofs.

Voller returned the compliment four minutes into the second half to lay on what proved to be the winner for Allofs.

Scotland 0 Uruguay 0

Scotland team: Leighton; Gough, Albiston, Nicol (Cooper 70), Miller, Narey, Strachan, McStay, Sharp, Aitken, Sturrock (Nicholas 70).

Remarkably, Scotland could still qualify with a win. Jose Batista was sent off early on for a wild challenge on Gordon Strachan but Uruguay dug deep to secure a stalemate.

Scotland did not create much but the best chance fell to Steve Nicol who missed from just six yards out after Strachan had set him up.

Alex Ferguson sent on Davie Cooper and Charlie Nicholas in an attempt to open up the Uruguay defence but it ended in frustration.

Italy 1990

Costa Rica 1 Scotland 0

Scotland team: Leighton; Gough (McKimmie 45), Malpas, Aitken, McLeish, McPherson, Bett (McCoist 74), McStay, Johnston, McCall, McInally.

Scotland under-performed in Genoa as Costa Rica became the first Central American team to win a match at the finals.

Juan Cayasso's 49th-minute strike when he lofted the ball over Jim Leighton after a back-heel from Jara proved enough to give Costa Rica their win.

Scotland did not muster much in response and it left them with an uphill struggle to qualify.

GENOA
10.6.90

SCOTTISH POLICE UNIT – QUESTURA GENOA

For the information and assistance(hopefully!) of all Scottish fans in Genoa.

The behaviour of Scots fans so far has been excellent and just what we expected. The local police are very pleased. Despite the large number of our Tartan Army in Genoa not one has been arrested. Two Dutchmen were arrested yesterday in possession of drugs and 4 English hooligans have been arrested and deported over the last two days. We are keeping a running total of arrests and are delighted to show our Italian colleagu the zero in the Scottish column each day – Keep up the good work!

Scotland 2 Sweden 1

Scotland team: Leighton; Levein, Malpas, Aitken, McLeish, McPherson, Fleck (McCoist 85), MacLeod, Johnston, McCall, Durie (McStay 75).

Andy Roxburgh made four changes with Craig Levein, Robert Fleck, Murdo MacLeod and Gordon Durie all coming in and it paid off.

Stuart McCall gave Scotland a 10th-minute lead from a flick by Dave McPherson and Mo Johnston scored late from the penalty spot after Roy Aitken was fouled by Roland Nilsson.

Glenn Stromberg, the Swedish substitute, pulled back a late goal but Scotland were worthy winners.

Brazil 1 Scotland 0

Scotland team: Leighton; McKimmie, Malpas, Aitken, McLeish, McPherson, McStay, MacLeod (Gillespie 38), Johnston, McCall, McCoist (Fleck 78).

Scotland bowed out of the competition in Turin after losing a painful late goal to the Brazilians.

Jim Leighton failed to hold a shot from Alemao and the ball ran loose for substitute Muller to poke home the only goal of the game after 81 minutes.

Mo Johnston and Ally McCoist were paired up front but Scotland did not create too much in front of goal.

SCOTLAND & THE WORLD CUP

France 1998

Brazil 2 Scotland 1

Scotland team: Leighton; Calderwood, Hendry, Boyd, Burley, Collins, Jackson (W McKinlay 78), Lambert, Dailly (T McKinlay 84), Durie, Gallacher.

Scotland, under Craig Brown, had the honour of opening the World Cup with holders Brazil.

Brazil scored after just four minutes when Cesar Sampaio turned in Bebeto's corner at the near post.

John Collins equalised from the penalty spot after Kevin Gallacher had been fouled and Scotland matched Brazil after that. But, after 73 minutes, Cafu's shot struck Jim Leighton and bounced off Tom Boyd into the net for the decisive goal.

Norway 1 Scotland 1

Scotland team: Leighton; Calderwood (Weir 59), Hendry, Boyd, Burley, Collins, Jackson (McNamara 61), Lambert, Dailly, Durie, Gallacher.

Norway had not lost for almost 18 months and Scotland knew the Bordeaux game would be difficult.

After stalemate in the first half, Norway drew first blood when Havard Flo headed in a cross from Vidar Riseth.

Craig Burley lobbed an equaliser after 66 minutes from a long through-ball from David Weir to keep Scotland's qualifying hopes alive.

Morocco 3 Scotland 0

Scotland team: Leighton; Weir, Hendry, Boyd, McNamara (T McKinlay 54), Lambert, Collins, Burley, Durie (Booth 84), Gallacher, Dailly.

Morocco put Scotland to the sword in emphatic style in St Etienne. Salaheddine Bassir volleyed a spectacular opening goal midway through the first half to leave Scotland up against it.

Abdeljalil Hadda scored the second after beating David Weir for pace two minutes into the second half before Craig Burley was sent off for a challenge on Bassir.

Scotland's misery was complete with six minutes left when Bassir scored his second goal.

SCOTLAND

SCOTLAND

Positional Quiz (page 16)

1 Jim Leighton – 91 caps between 1982-98.

2 Alan Rough (53) and Jim Leighton (91).

3 David Harvey.

4 Frank Haffey.

5 Andy Goram.

6 Alex McLeish (77).

7 Dundee United, Rangers and Tottenham Hotspur.

8 Tom Boyd.

9 51.

10 Gary Caldwell.

11 Both players won 54 international caps.

12 Paul McStay (76).

13 Lithuania in a European Championships qualifier in 1998.

14 John Wark.

15 Craig Burley – v Norway at France '98.

16 Ally McCoist – v Switzerland.

17 Luxembourg in a European Championships qualifier in 1986.

18 One – in Germany '74.

19 England, in May 1973.

20 Four.

Let's Get Quizical (page 32)

1 David Clarkson

2 Christophe Berra

3 Kenny Miller, against Croatia.

4 Stephen McManus

5 Craig Gordon, Paul Hartley and Kenny Miller.

6 Luca Toni and Christian Panucci.

7 Barry Ferguson.

8 Shaun Maloney and Garry O'Connor.

9 Lee McCulloch.

10 Darren Fletcher.

11 Garry O'Connor.

12 South Africa.

13 Allan McGregor.

14 Kenny Miller.

15 Andy Webster.

16 Brazil – in 1974, 1982, 1990 and 1998.

17 1954 – in Switzerland.

18 Joe Jordan – in 1974, 1978 and 1982.

19 Zaire.

20 Craig Brown – France 1998.

Word Search

Page 17

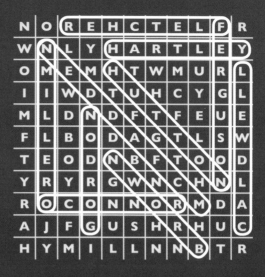

Page 33

WHEREVER IT TAKES US